OLD STORIES
SOME NOT TRUE

OLD STORIES
SOME NOT TRUE
and other poems

Tim Gillespie

MoonPath Press

Poetry
ISBN 978-1-936657-51-3

Cover photo by Janine Sprout

Back cover author photo by Jan Giske Gillespie

Interior author photo by Jenna Gillespie

Book design by Tonya Namura, using Malaga Narrow OTCE.

MoonPath Press is dedicated to publishing the finest poets living in the U.S. Pacific Northwest.

MoonPath Press
PO Box 445
Tillamook, OR 97141

MoonPathPress@gmail.com

http://MoonPathPress.com

To those millennia of storytellers, griots, poets, bards, skalds,
minstrels, jelis, songwriters, and shanachies
who have cared about true words:
I hope I have listened well enough

Contents

Old Stories, Some Not True

A Peaceful Uproar

Finding Direction

Green moss
spills down
the bark.
"That's the north side,"
I say eagerly,
ready to show what I've heard:
how not to get lost.
"No," says my Scoutmaster,
squatting with his compass,
eyeballing the sky.
"That's an old story
and not always true."

The years spill down
past old stories,
some not true.
Sky, bark, you,
needle dancing north,
moss off a bough.
What I'd give
to get lost now.

Seven or Seventy Wonders of a City

"You take delight not in a city's seven or seventy wonders,
but in the answer it gives to a question of yours."
~ Italo Calvino, *Invisible Cities*

I read somewhere once that people with Scots-Irish ancestry like me aren't settled until we've lived in three different places in our lives, perhaps reflecting the historic migration of our forebears from Scotland to Northern Ireland to North America.

My father fit the stereotype, a city boy from Omaha who lit out as a young man for Minneapolis and later headed to Los Angeles to start his family.

And to my surprise when I stumbled over that pebble of generalization, I fit the pattern, too. I grew up in Alhambra, one of the oldest towns abutting Los Angeles, then trekked north to the San Francisco Bay area for a few years, and ended up starting a family with my wife after we'd decamped even farther north to Portland, Oregon, migrating city to city to city.

This section locates poems in those three places—the city streets and houses of my wanderings, the gardens and homesteads of my landings.

I.

"Aesthetics is for the artist as
ornithology is for the birds."
~ Barnett Newman

That Day at the Hat Shop

I take the MAX train downtown, jump the trolley,
end up on NW 23rd, strolling the street,
watching the crowd-wad, but my old head is cold.
It's a deep-winter day, trees stripped of leaves
and sun out, but brisker than I've expected.
In the absence of natural thatch, the freak flag
of my youth a long-gone memory, me bare topside—
you can't grow grass on a busy street, my old man
used to say, and—*those keratoses aren't unsightly,*
my apparently 19-year-old dermatologist told me,
let's just call them your wisdom spots, dear—dang, my
noggin is freezing, and all this fine ruminating
is not warming the cranium. Thinking slowly
as I am, I pass a small hat shop, walk by, stop
a half-block up the street, turn around, go back.
A small tinkle announces my entrance, which
puts me in mind that I ought to find a restroom
sometime soon. *Good day,* says the hip-hatted mook
at the counter with a beard halfway to his waist,
twice what I used to have when I was his age. *Just
looking to heat up the braincase, young man.*
He nods. I try on fedoras and flatcaps, berets
and gatsbys and outbacks, and finally find
a newsboy cap that fits my noodle, pull out
my wallet, plop down my dough. The kid's got
his eyeballs all over my dome. *That lid
looks particularly good on you, pop,* he says. *I'm
not* particular, I say. *When it comes to form
and function, I don't need aesthetic arguments,
I just want some warmth to thaw the wits.*

II.

"Where did we come from,
what happens next?"
~ Margaret Atwood,
The Telegraph

The Screen

Just east of East L.A., early 1960's

Those nights of rainbirds chattering on the lawns,
I'd try, my nose against the window screen, to find
the quiet scents of mock orange, bougainvillea,
lemons ripening on the tree at Old Man Shonerock's
next door on the downhill side, or sometimes
his sweet pipesmoke on the air, and on my old t-shirt
the residue of summer days: fresh-mown grass
and sweat, a sniff of suntan oil, and barbeque
from up the hill at Tookie's house that afternoon.

I'd stretch the wrong way on the bed, feet on my pillow,
up on my elbows, chin cradled in palms, just to stare
long hours out the window, face against the screen
to find whatever breeze might faintly stir across
that L.A. heat, and hear the sirens flying toward
some hurt, and see the sky smeared by the last streak
of daylight—a smog sky, red as blood or salsa.
My crystal radio set crackled softly, playing
rock & roll or Vin Scully calling Dodger games.
Through the dented screen I saw the world stretch
down the ridge, across the valley, back up
to Elephant Hill, where we'd hiked as kids
and at the top stared through the haze
to City Hall downtown, a scant seven miles away,
our dad had said. One time up there we found
a hobo camp, and ran home down the hill,
afraid of the ragged, footloose murderers
of our imaginations in the City of Angels.
Then some developer shaved that hill
and threw a thousand houses up.

Stretched out backwards on the rumpled bed,
I'd look out at the lights on those hot nights,

imagining them as secret messages
from all those homes splayed over the hill,
and voices floated on the air—low, indistinct—
of people murmuring secrets I'd imagine,
their windows also open to the heat,
and other radios were on with other tunes,
the crack of Dodger bats, the roaring crowds.

But mostly I remember through the dusty,
dinged-up screen of time the bobbing lights,
a blur of white and red across the I-10 freeway
that ran eight lanes along the valley floor,
motorsong magnified in the still summer air.
I could hear the trucks come down Garvey Ave,
downshifting, compression braking, sighing
with their loads. At night, still packed, the freeway
roared with engine hum and tire hiss, and I'd
imagine it a river, whose ceaseless stream
flowed downroad on and on, a thousand
thousand cars all swept and pushed and drawn
somewhere far off that screen's small frame. Where,
where could they all be going so late at night?
I could not imagine, could only sigh, shift,
and roar away to someplace else.

The Homemade Pipe Organ in Movay's Garage

Danny Movay, who'd cracked open
Victor-across-the-street's head with a rock
during neighborhood combat, slouched
down Snead Drive, angry king of the block
in his torn-up tennies and face.
Down the street around the corner
we'd walk by the Movay place
hoping on weekends the garage door
would be sprung so we could glance
the metal pipes all upright in a row
like Marlboros in their pack,
and wooden pipes lined up by rank.

Danny's old man in his ash-pocked t-shirt,
always with a smoke crammed in his mug
and quick with a knuckle to his son's head,
would tell us most days *scram, you punks*.
But sometimes in the summers he'd
be cutting pipe or sanding wood
and would stoop to talk to older boys
of pistons, stop-knobs, wind chests, valves,
and how pitch changes with the weather.

And then one night, through my window
thrown up against deep August's swelter,
I heard an airy hum, and then the crash
and bellow of the organ, pipes full-throated,
and pictured, ciggie at his lip, Dan's dad,
squinting through the smoke, pounding keys,
changing the pitch of the Snead Drive eve,
and Danny too listening in bed. That music
cracked open my head.

Why You'd Drive to San Clemente

Boardwalk
Seagull squawk
Oyster stew
Wavetalk

Sandal thwap
Saltair smack
Pigeon coo
Tanned back

Ocean roil
Suntan oil
Pierside blue
Boy, girl

Shakes

at Temptations Ice Cream Shoppe
on Valley Boulevard, Alhambra, California, 1966

I paid for the two shakes
with a buck I'd saved
from edging lawns.

Walking back from the counter
(two tall glasses in hand,
chocolate in one,
strawberry in the other,
in my fingers two paper straws
and two long spoons
against the icy glass),
I edged into the seat
across from her
in the red vinyl booth
and thought of the movie
malt shop scene
where the boy and girl
lean over one shake
with their two straws.

But that was not
this trip to Temptations.
Something was sticky,
an edge to the scene.
She slurped, I
had cold hands.
My straw sucked flat.
Pink strawberry slid
down her fluted glass.

The Bike on the Porch
"Grief is the final act of love."
~ Caitlin Flanagan

I won't forget riding my Schwinn,
pack on my back, wheeling off
with my crew to the park for the day,
racing down the hill past the sad house
three blocks over with blinds always drawn
and the front light on night and day
and a rusted bicycle propped on the porch.

Our posse had all heard the story
of the sad family. Whisper was
they'd lost their little boy to leukemia
and couldn't bear to take his bike
from the porch where it waited—
kickstand up, leaned against the siding
of the sad house, summer and winter,
waiting, ready, for the boy's next ride.

We'd whoosh quickly by that house,
trying not to glance at the bike on the porch,
reminder of a riderlessness far beyond
our understanding, sorrow being
a weight that others bore. And two
blocks on, we were back to laughter,
shouting, up on our pedals, kids heedless
and free, the sting of the wind in our eyes,
speeding to the park, ready.

Ten years on, my own little brother,
swooping down the steepest hill
in our hometown, lost control,
and we lost him in a tangle of bike and bus.

1

I won't forget that porch light always
dimly on. I want to knock on that door
and tell those folks inside, don't keep
the bike on the porch. Walk it to the street,
get on, force the balky gears, climb the hill,
turn and scream down it, the sting of wind
in your eyes. You want to soar,
you're going to weep.

III.

"I'm willing to be moving."
            ~ Little Feat, "Willing"

Crossroads Blues

I went down to the crossroads, took a look from west to east.
Out the west way lived the woman who'd laid out a sit-down feast.
If I walked toward that sweet sunset, knew my rootless days would cease.

So I ambled to the east fork, gazed a long time down that road,
Saw the freedom of my rambling, saw the unknown and the bold.
At the crossroads sat the question: Do I gamble? Do I hold?

Now I look back at that turning, many miles down the way,
And I cannot have regrets about that long-gone crossroads day.
We take what roads we take, babe. Let the moondogs sit and bay.

Spider Plant

I was looking for a birthday gift to snugly fit our mood
the way that laces sometimes groove old boots.
And then I found a spider plant; I saw us in its sprouts—
like them we're stretched away from ground and roots.

The spidersprout leaves home when young, it hitchhikes off in space,
expands itself in fitful spurts and zooms
until it's taut with tension, pinched and strained—it begs to snap,
stretched far as it can reach, and there it blooms.

Housewarming

May God bless this home
and may the windowpanes sing in the sun
the roof beams settle, smug in their brawn
the floorboards groan in unpolished pleasure
the nails hold sure, snug in their grip

May the teapot toot stoutly when it's coming to port
the faucets pour out their gurgling hearts
the flap on the postbox get snarky re: junk mail
the broom and the pan tsk tsk over dust
the bedroom keep secrets, the kitchen spill beans

May the fir tree sway in a windborne waltz
the alarm clock dance in a wake-'em-up samba
the foundation stay stoic, the gutters gargle regularly
the cheeks of the fireplace grin at the heat
the front door open wide and say ahh

And may the joists and the jambs, the drainpipes and lights
the bannisters, doorknobs, porch steps, and plants
the casements and toaster and fridge-nestled beer
in a chorus shout welcome we're happy
you're here

IV.

"More grows in the garden than
the gardener sows."
~ Spanish proverb

Yardwork

In my father's ordered yard
I labored long along the well-
oiled clippers' blades.
In the adolescent sway
between my father's cultivation
and constraint, and my nature,
I sweated revolution,
daydreamed uproots and uprisings.
Under sullen obligations
of the mower and the rake,
I keenly cut and quietly raged
for yards gone unrestrained,
a patch of blooming chaos,
tall as grain, untended, rank.

Now I like a trim yard.
But my well-clippped, once-wild heart
still sometimes beats a protest:
Let it bloom, let it
grow, let it slip!
I prune. I mow. I clip.

End of the Season

I've been out raking leaves.
The piles are finally in the street.
Thin branches of the weeping birch
hang down above the leaf-free sidewalk
where I inspect my work.
On one branchtip, the last
frail birch leaf hangs—brown,
shrivelled, parchment-dry. I perch
the rake a half-inch off my shoulder.
My stance is wide, rake
poised with two tight hands
choked up on it, right elbow
jutting sharply out, left
elbow in. I glare
a moment at the leaf
that curves there in the air.
I take my cut, rake
whistling as my wrists snap.
(It clears the fence,
the season's last home run.)

The Idea of Order in Winter

At the Lan Su Chinese Garden
amid the Scholar's Courtyard peace,
they've named the yardstone pattern
Plum blossoms on cracked ice.

At home, in my garden,
in January's cold and grey,
I can't discern a pattern.
I squat and squint. I name:

Leaf glop on mulchmound.
Pavingstones slowly uprooting.
Lamb's ears flattened.
Daphne buds waiting.

Spirea naked and swaying.
Wind gust and twig tremble.
Fat clumps of mushrooms hiding.
A grapevine tangle.

Leaf mold and last rose.
Green lichenblooms on the maples.
Ferment and woodsmoke.
Furled leaves in rain puddles.
Squirrel chatter, crow squawk.
Raspberry brambles.

Mildew smears down fence slats.
Moss tufts and bark peel.
Sweetgum-thrown seedpods.
Rough callused branch cuts.
Fountaingrass quivering, hellebore silence.
Paint peel and black branches. Clinging clematis.
Last gasp ajuga scrubby and dank.

Decay and rankness. Fern furl and
deadwood and mudsmear
and chaos and rot.

Oh, blessed rage for order.
Behold our human composition.
Meanwhile anarchy gathers itself.
The garden stirs in opposition.

Steller's Jay

Blue blur
at eye edge. I,
book-bound, look, spot the jay, fat
on a fir bough, squawking.
Bird blab.

Murder in the Cherry Tree

It's late May, early morning. I pull the windowblind cord
to check out the cherries erupting on my backyard tree. But,
rubbing my eyes, I see a dark dilemma pecking at the fruit.

See, crows thrive on our street. My neighbor befriends them,
names them, leaves food scraps on his porch rail. All I know
of crows is angry cawing, the swoop of black wings overhead,
vast gobs of crowsplat on my driveway from their perch
on the powerline stretching above. Then there's that ominous
raven on Poe's bust of Pallas that croaks *nevermore*.

They're not the same, my neighbor says, an expert
on *Corvus*: the genus of crows, ravens, jackdaws, and rooks.
Crows rattle and caw, he tells me. Ravens gronk, deeper
and throatier, and chuckle sometimes. Ravens run larger,
have beards, travel in pairs. Crows are crowned with
fluffs of feathers, mohawked lads that run in larger murders.
Ravens like the woods; crows are city birds. Ours: definitely crows.

But you feed them? I ask. These angry birds? They're smart,
he says. They can use tools. They memorize the routes
of garbage trucks, following the promise of sweet trashspill.
Crow language has regional dialects. We probably have
our own street's crow slang. They recognize our upturned faces,
he says, and remember them. They hold grudges, repay kindness,
and teach their tribe to do the same over generations.

Armed with my new knowledge, hoping to save my progeny
from generational crow-feud, I stop arguing with the crows
on my street and trying to scare them off with a stomp of my foot.
I start talking to them: *Don't worry, crow, I mean you no harm. We can
co-exist here. Enjoy your feast of smashed something on the street.*
And soon they soon stop cawing at me. We become familiars,
neighbors not close but respectful, just like Marv kitty-corner

across the street. Though I can't recognize the crows well enough
to name them yet, I do know the lame one who bounces across lawns
on one spindly leg, the other tucked up and useless. Hoppy, I call him.

But this May morning, yawning and stretching, I open the back blinds,
see violent tugging in the cherry tree. It's only a few days till harvest,
and those frickin' birds are beaking the fruit off the tree—even Hoppy!—
stripping delicious dark cherries in their prime. That's not right.
That's not neighborly. I throw on my yardboots, ready to go out
and yell at them, shoo them off. *Hey! What are you doing?*
Get out of my tree! But then, I pause: I'll lose my new pals.
And they'll be screeching at me, or their children will, and
their grandchildren, for the rest of my life. *Evermore.*
So here's the dilemma: harmony or harvest?

Backyard Bargaining

Ah, raucous cawing crow, would you
exchange that cunning brain
for a better singing voice?

And you, wee whir of hummingbird,
if you had a choice, would you
choose to trade that speedy blur
for a chill-out aptitude?

And twitchy squirrel pal, would you
swap that daring high wire skill
for a better squish-evading street sense?

And you, red-shafted flicker, pesky
phonepole pecker, would you
ever drop those drumming chops
to exist for a minute in the bliss
of a headache-free hush?

Ah, backyard friends, are you, like us,
disposed to disappointment, steeped
in hopes of magic metamorphoses?
Do you bargain with your gods as we do—
squawking, darting, tightrope-walking,
banging your heads as hard against
the way things are in the yard?

Dirtwork: The Spring Campaign

I scrape from the raised bed the winter-rot,
my escape from the canker of politics inside,
then rake in manure, mulch-ready the garden box,
a break from the rancor and shit of the news.

I divide the dug-up dahlia bulbs of last fall,
fortify the dark soil, replant the bulbs in the reek,
pulverize any dirt clods, tamp down my ire,
and side with the tubers biding their time.

Later I tug off in the basement my mud-boots,
trudge upstairs, take root at my desk,
slug out letters to editors, sign petitions,
join the scrum and the spew of that world.

I'm aggrieved by this truth: as my soil now
needs amending, so does the world's hard ground.
The tea kettle boils and howls to be heeded.
The garden needs tending. I'm breeding just outrage.

My nudgings of nature in my little earth-patch
leave gunk under my nails, dirt-smutch and blood.
The crud and the blight on TV seeps deeper—
hard to scrub, toxic, ceaseless, dumb.

I know rage can overgrow joy in the garden,
take hold—relentless weed—if it's nurtured and fed,
but oh, when I'm readying my last box of dirt,
let me be sowing dahlias instead.

V.

"You must be able to walk firmly on the ground before you start walking on a tightrope."

~ Henri Matisse

On Sandy Boulevard

I'm   walking up Sandy,
the   only diagonal road
in the   orderly perpendicularity
of the   street grid of my neighborhood.

Amid   weed dispensaries
and fast   food drive-thru joints,
food cart   pods, coffee shops,
gyms, and   karaoke taverns,
a stream of   cars churns by
on the gash   of this street.

I've heard the   thoroughfare follows
the course of an   ancient path
ground to sand by   hide-clad feet,
a time-worn route   of Chinookan peoples
traversing Columbia   to Willamette, a
shortcut from river to   river.

This portageway linked   for long centuries
rich fishing spots, Celilo   Falls to Whilamut Falls,
the car-spawning road of   today hewing to that
history of trade and travel,   though those cataracts
are long gone, dammed up   now and well-tamed,
the street an anomaly, the old   scar cut across our
invasion of condos and graph-   papered streets.

I walk up the slow rise of Sandy   Boulevard, and
the buildings and billboards fall   away, the concrete
dissolves, the truck roar and car   fumes and road rush all
fade. There's promise of potlatch   and dust of the trail in my mouth.

Ross Hollywood Chapel in Spring

Two burly young bucks, white-coated,
burst out the back door of the mortuary,
perch on the parking lot curb to have a smoke.
I'm striding by on a shortcut home
from the post office on the busy street
that bisects this old city neighborhood,
over-woven with century trees, root-sprung
sidewalks underfoot, kids' bikes stacked on porches
on a late-April day rent by the eruptions of spring.
A strand of smoke curls from the chapel chimneystack.

I've just walked my handful of mail to the P.O.,
letters to old friends, messages to past lives,
slipped them through the slot, am ambling homeward,
alert to the riotous blossoming around me, all
promise and earth-push: a yard-patch of heuchera
erupting in purple, bronze, amber, and chocolate,
and rhodies and roses, tulips and peonies, dark-bearded
pansies, unfurling fiddleheads, all shout *I'm here.*

The mortuary guys and I make quick eye contact
as I walk by, then we all look away, sideways or up
into the thin blue firmament and the fact of that smoke.
Cremation and germination: a joke and a juke
in the spring-ripe air. Messages are being
dispatched. *You're here, you're gone.*
Here.

Out on a Record-Breaking Warm Saturday in January

The shocking day: the sun blinding, gloves
crammed in my pocket, jacket over my arm,
steam rising from the drying-out, early
flowering viburnum and daphne in the air—
a bounty so unexpected, a slap of joy.

"Beautiful day," I say to a woman digging
in her yard. We've nodded other times when
I've walked by her house a half-mile from mine.
"Yes," she says, "unseasonably warm," brushing back
a strand of hair with her muddy glove. "I wonder
what it means, though," she says, her trowel
plunging into the dirt, "and if we should worry."

The what-it-means: glacial melting, coral
reefs bleached of life, tsunami and storm surge,
rising seas swamping small villages, drought
looming and fire and mudslide to follow—
a small scent of wintersweet punches my nose.

City Nature

Greasy rainbows
in the street.

Green and red and yellow
on a tall stalk of steel.

A thousand
trees. No forest.

The Scrape

Out the door with my old pal Steve on a weekday city walk,
we amble northeast, yakking all the way, a three-mile jaunt
to a brewery on Northeast Dekum Street, just down the block
from Woodlawn Park, which used to be and may be still—
what do I know?—turf of the Bloods, but nowadays the park's
benign, at least before night falls. A mom and her kids chuck
a ball around. A guy with tattoos up his arms walks his dog.
This corner of town gentrifies at the speed of white, it's called,
so two retired old honkies can safely stroll and blithely talk.
Something's gained, I guess, but so much lost: black
churches shuttered, front porches empty of the elders, folks
forced out to The Numbers by soaring rents and prices. It breaks
my heart, but here I am in the middle of it. This street has lost
a measure of poverty's grief and harm, it's true, but more's the pain
of a neighborhood of ghosts that used to be a community.

So we get to the brewpub, have a sandwich—Cubano for me,
veggie wrap for Steve—and a pint from the tap—IPA for him
and me a pils. The lunch crowd is bike riders, hipsters, nose-ringed
laptop jockeys. "Doesn't anyone have a job anymore?" asks Steve.

On the walk home Steve asks what I've been writing. I pull out
my cell because I've got some poems in there, and I'm walking
and gabbing and scrolling to find one to read to my poor captive chum.
You know what they say about distracted driving, yeah? Well, clearly
we also need fair warnings regarding distracted walking because
my foot—expecting *terra firma*—finds instead a vacancy, a divot in
the crumbling concrete of the old sidewalk that turns my ankle
and sends me spilling forward, and when my skid comes to a halt,
my knee and shin are an angry grit-packed strawberry oozing blood
as thick as any scrape I've had since I was a kid and went flying off
my skateboard trying to impress Esther Ruiz down the street

as she sat on a wall coolly smoking in my old neighborhood
east of East L.A. And Lord, whatever happened to Esther Ruiz
and those old streets with their own ghosts and cracks?

Well...blood, grit, hurt, remembrance, loss—this the cost
of finding a poem on Northeast Dekum Street.

Fine Grind

at a coffee shop on N.E. Fremont Street, Portland

I'm deep in my work, notebook out, late afternoon,
oblivious to the java-fueled hubbub around me until
that big voice booms out: "What's crackin', kid?"

I'm dragged from my work: a boy in a baseball cap
folding his ears down, shoulders hunched, sits leaning in,
head on the arm of what looks to be his mom. Then
striding across the coffee shop comes Mr. Enthusiastic
who gives the kid a hug, which the boy takes looking away
but folding himself into the big tattooed arms. I note:
the mom's ringless finger and fretful look, the kid's small smile
trembling somewhere between hope and trepidation, and
Mr. E's loud charm, and try to read the scene: Single mom
readying the handoff to a Big Brother for her dad-deprived boy?
Nah. Single mom passing her son off for an overnighter
to slightly scary and perpetually stoned Uncle Billy,
who's always fun but God knows lacks all good sense?
Could be, but as they talk and Mr. E broadcasts across
the caffeinated air his sympathy for all the hard choices
they all have to make in this difficult time, and his trust
that the kid will make the right one since he's shown everyone
what a cool dude he is, and so smart, and such a good fielder,
I land on another possibility, which I want to be wrong about,
while Mr. E does all the talking, looking over the kid's head,
and the boy stares at the floor littered with muffin crumbs,
and mom seems close to dissolving in latte foam, and now I think
this is dad after the splintering, and the cosmos is flying apart
for this trying-to-be-brave little boy who has to decide
whom he'll live with when all that he wants is the way it was,
and this awful choice has to happen in the neutral ground
of the coffee shop, while the barista yells someone's name

and the espresso machine hisses, and everyone in the joint
is an unwilling witness. Please God grant that I've misread
the whole situation and this whole poem's a mispour.

But look at your little boy, buddy.
What's crackin'? His heart.

Inscription

LOVE hung below the overpass
in yellow spraypaint,
a sunny smear on a concrete post,
the freeway grey and loud above.
Just LOVE—a blunt commandment,
wish, smug manifesto, dream,
vow, spunky hope...an act:
paint fast, then cut and run.

For two years on this squat abutment
LOVE was stuck
without a lover's name, no date,
no heart or other body parts,
no "Call 286-1191"—
just LOVE, just
bright generic LOVE.

And then the city must've sent
a crew to scrub it off.
LOVE disappeared
for some sound civic principle:
to save the public from the glut,
the danger, warning, funk, disorder,
the dumb and disrespectful
stunning spray of LOVE.

A Winter's Grace

Late night walk,
chill winter air.
Over the treetops—
look, over there:

Full moon—still,
poised above trees,
haloed with ice,
silver, at peace.

Pause. Watch the moon
halted mid-flight,
held in the hands
of the clouds this night.

May we be held
in the dark of our lives,
poised in the breath
of luminous light.

Old Stories,
Some Not True

The poems in this next section have all been sparked in one way or another by the flint and steel of old stories—myths, legends, fables, books, plays—and shavings of history.

Many of these poems are informed by my years as an English teacher in public schools, trying to help students find solace, provocation, insight, and themselves in stories.

I.

"The beginnings and endings of all
human undertakings are untidy..."
~ John Galsworthy,
Over the River

What Shall I Sing?

Shy cowherd Cædmon, barn-bound, sang
brave hymns among his animals. Hay
pile pews shone in the slant light:
cattle-low, pigeon-coo, and sheep-bleat
his earthly choir. The abbey monks
would laugh, the stable stench no seemly
site for holy song, old stiff Cædmon
no cantor, just the farm hand who could
not read yet sang to straw and slop.
Amid the shit and squawk, our first poet's home,
old Cædmon faced the fearsome angel, from
his mouth sang of the mighty maker, architect
who'd blessed all below the heavenly roof
with all its laughter, bellow, stink and hoof.

II.

"It is worth our while in the confusions and
bewilderments of the present to consider the
way by which the Greeks arrived at the clarity
of their thought and the affirmation of their art."
~ Edith Hamilton, *The Greek Way*

Daphne by the Front Steps

Third year in-ground, the branch-twined daphne
perches by the front steps, quiet and gnarled, unnoticed.
But three Februarys now, on unexpected days (me
just home in haste-worn, what's-next mode,
bag of work in one hand, coat-hunched against the cold),
the daphne announces herself. Grabs my eye and nose
like a troll at the steps demanding an off-season toll.
I'm shrub-stunned, slammed to pause by the tiny,
surprising four-fold buds, first-bloom, so lone
and delicate the pink-red dab against the grey of winter's
reach. But it's the scent—slight, sweet—that follows me
up the steps and into my house and marrowbone.

The old tale of Daphne trails along, too,
from a long-ago library's book of Greek myths:
Apollo-mocked, Eros drew his bow, unquivered two arrows,
one gold to kindle love, one repellant lead.
The boy knew the crowing Sun God was sweet on Daphne,
river-nymph. So, he pulled and sent the lead-nosed fletch,
and evermore the forest-roaming girl would find love's pull
abhorrent. Then Eros shot Apollo's heart with arrow-gold,
to long forever then for what he never could have, the
wood-waif Daphne. But dauntless, love-stuck, mush-head gone,
he chased her, hound on hare, around the rills and stones.
She fled, ran through the woods, called "Leave me be,"
pled to the gods, "Save me from love's mad boundless mess."
The gods heard her lament, changed her to a tree, root-grown
into the rocky ground. Form-changed, she bloomed.
Apollo moaned. And there grew Daphne,
ever sought and ever sweet, alone.

Inside my house, at my wide desk, the scent faint yet in nose,
I check the hefty garden book for Daphne. Here's the entry:
Daphne odora, bloom of not-spring, surprise of winter,

whose smell is evanescent. But leave it be, the book says,
exercise wariness; the plant is highly toxic.
This, the blessing and the woe of sweetness
that we can't quite ever catch and hold.

The Old Men of Argos

The old men of Argos,
warriors no more
(left behind when the Greeks,
puffed up, sailed to Troy,
their thousand-craft armada
packed with an army
of armor clad men-boys),
stood slack-armed on shore
as those ships slipped to sea,
and stared at each other,
grey-bearded and bent with regret.

But these displaced old war-gods
could still thump their chests
in cane-steadied chorus: "Well,
the gods have bestowed on us
new fighting strengths—
the spear of persuasion, the
power of song, the age-honed
eloquence to spin stories
that stir and provoke."

The moral this tale tells:
Old peacocks still honk. And yet,
those ancient boys were onto something:
arguments do outlive armadas,
songs swords, stories strong-arms.

Trojan Horse with Orange Mane

Epeius was the crafter
of the beast and a Greek
soldier, boxing champ, and
master carpenter—a deviser
and destroyer.

From far-off city walls we watched, perplexed,
as he steamed and bent planks of fir for ribs,
peg-joined the belly staves atop stout legs,
added neck and warhorse head, bored eyeholes
that he fit with wine-red amethysts, cast
bronze hooves, added wheels, then wove
gold-spangled cloth strips for the mane,
strewed the saddle pad with jewels, braided
the reins with purple flowers, all to blind
us to what was hollow, what lurked inside.

Epeius stood back and
beheld the majesty
and treachery he'd made,
beheld what we were willing
to roll inside our gates.

Cassandra in Three Acts

Act I: The Trophy

Haughty in his narrow victory at Troy,
the mighty King of Argos, Agamemnon
(genius general of the hollow wooden horse,
the jeweled, gold-pocked façade of which concealed
the violence huddled inside, waiting in the dark),
took when he won what he thought he deserved.
"You can do anything," he said, "when you're a star."
Part of his loot-grab was Cassandra, the dark-skinned
royal daughter of the slaughtered Trojan tribe,
his trophy concubine—"...a woman," she keened,
"sinking in a sea of child-men." Old Agamemnon
wanted her to prove his might, and also craved
to have her use her gift to see his fate.

Act II: Her Gift

Cassandra was the same girl in earlier years chased
and twice-cursed by Apollo. Drawn by her light,
the Sun God too had moved on her—you can do
anything when you're a star—and lured her
with a shiny bauble. That glittery gift: to see the future.
Attracted by the trinket, she'd given up a covert kiss,
but when Apollo pressed for more, she pushed him off.
Rebuffed, the Sun God thrust on her a second gift
that cursed the first: thenceforth, whatever fate
the girl foresaw would never be believed. And so
down through the tidal shifts of time, Cassandra lives on,
the one who tries to sing of danger, who warns of what
we can't or won't foresee, who drowns in desperate knowledge
of the seas of sorrow still to come but clings to hope
her song will find a shore, though no one listens.

Act III: Cassandra Redux

Tonight my granddaughter is Cassandra
in the production at her high school of the *Oresteia,*
Aeschylus' ancient recounting of this timeworn tale.
She plays the role committed to that desperate,
urgent Trojan girl. At 16, Shawnie understands
Cassandra's madness, the hurt of being unheard,
the cruelty and attraction of Apollo's cocksure charm,
the devastation of a tribe's diminishment. She gets
the sting at being dismissed for being a girl; for being
too young, too smart; for having darker skin; for holding
fiercely to her trust that there are truths that can be known.
When preening men of power who think they're stars or suns
offer you a curse they claim is a gift, she knows: resist.
They can't just *do anything.* Let them be forewarned
that here's a girl who won't be grabbed except by truths
she won't stop telling, that here's a girl who won't
be lured by hollow jeweled things, that this girl's
no one's trophy, this girl's fate is not to go unheard.
No, Shawn, we need to hear. We might
believe you this time. Sing it.

Attic Ads

found plastered to the walls of an ancient Greek ruin of my imagination

The Procrustes B & B
"Home of the Perfect Bed"
Come stay with us...
you'll fit right in!

Tantalus Wines
Visit our tasting room. Quench your thirst.
Perfect luscious grapes and artisan spring water
conspire to make our vintage wines a tempting treat.
Check the prices on our products:
You may think they're out of reach,
but you'd be wrong again and again.

Arachne Sewing Shop
Threads to rival the gods!
Catch us on the web!

Icarus Skydiving School
Free yourself from your
humdrum cubicle.
Try a flight with our patented
feather-light parachute.
Perfect for a sunny day's
adventure in the sky.

The Phaeton Driving Academy
Learn to handle even
the trickiest of vehicles.

Pandora's House of Chests
Open one of our lovingly
hand-crafted, beautifully-fitted gift boxes
and wonder at what you've found
and wonder at what you've done.

The Antikythera Mechanism: A Lecture

In ancient days, in the Aegean Sea, off the coast
of the tiny goat-clotted Greek isle of Antikythera,
a ship sank, then sat sea-bedded 2,000 years till spotted
in the tidal swirl a century ago by sponge-divers.
At the deepest reach of diving safety, the wreck
was slowly looted of its merchant treasure:
statue heads and arms of bronze and marble,
long-necked amphorae stacked near glass-tiled bowls
unbroken by the surge and jolt of centuries of sea-roil.
I read about this as a kid, and dived deep.

The storm-sunk cargo ship of luxury goods,
sailing, scholars think, from Rhodes to Rome,
its hold of treasure sent perhaps to gild the pomp
of a parade for Julius Caesar, offered up one mystery
amid the trove of jewelry and coins for trumpeting
the time-battered banality of a tyrant's power-strut:
this one unfathomable lump of bronze—corroded,
encased in brined gunk once a wooden box—the size
of Grandpa's mantel clock. I wish I'd been the one
to swim that sea-gift to the surface.

This dust-gathering glob then sat shelf-bound
another half century till someone pulled it down,
peeled apart the lump, and through the crust of time
and salt discovered discs and spindle fragments,
clockwork-like wood teeth of interlocking gears.
X-rays found a dial divided in degrees and dim
inscriptions to decipher. I think of Miss Ruzgarian's
mechanical orrery in third grade science that spun
the earth and moon in orbit-dance around the sun.
Entranced, I'd crank its handle till Miss R said, "Stop!"

The Antikythera Mechanism was that rig's long-lost kin.
From behind the rust and barnacles, an astronomical clock
emerged. You'd turn a knob, and slowly seven hands would
arc across its face. It tracked the motion of the sun and moon
adjusted for orbital irregularities, the variations in their
speeds at perigee and apogee, and all five planets visible to our
forebears' naked eyes plowing through the star-congested sky.
The gizmo marked the phases of the moon, eclipses years away,
a calendar of quadrennial festivals and games. I gape amazed at
the aspirations of the ancient crafters of this ecliptic contraption.

But the scholars say the apparatus isn't all that accurate,
its engineering lagging way behind its bold conceptions.
Still, older by a thousand years than any other gadget
ever found of such complex ambition, it bears wave-worn
witness to vast knowledge and inventiveness lost in depths
of time and sea. I envision some old mechanically-minded Greek
astronomer-poets watching the stars swirl overhead, imagining
the universe a grand machine predictably proceeding through
a cosmos understandable, crafting what they saw to human size,
a prize for despots primed to clutch the world in their small hands.

So, what have we learned? First, what ancient makers cast
in bronze not only ordered all the glories of the sky they saw,
but ordered how we still see them. Second, what we can conceive
laps the limits of what we can make. Third, parades of tyrants are a
long tradition. Fourth, the flaws in our trajectories are predictable.
Fifth, there's no smooth upward arc of progress. So earth-plunked,
we can only keep an eye turned skyward, crank the mechanisms
of our dreams, accommodate the wobbles in our orbits,
and try to line up with the imperfect stars.

III.

"I tried to imagine myself a long time ago, in the lands where these stories were first told during the long winter nights perhaps, under the glow of the northern lights, or sitting outside in the small hours, awake in the unending daylight of midsummer, with an audience of people who wanted to know what else Thor did, and what the rainbow was, and how to live their lives, and where bad poetry comes from."

~ Neil Gaiman, *Norse Mythology*

Two Ravens

The old Norse tale says one-eyed Odin
sent two ravens into the world each day—
one named Thought, one Memory—
to report back on news from Midgard where
those mystifying mortals carried on.

The ravens winged the world, scavenging
for carrion, death their first feast, scanning
with far-seeing eyes and hidden ears for all
the raw gut-spilling loves and follies of
those fathomless life-flattened humans.

Then barrel-rolling home in glee at what they'd
seen and heard, mocking as they flew the dull-voiced
songs and stories of those sorry earthbound beings,
soaring through the clouds digesting all that gritty gossip,
the birds returned to fertile Asgard and for Odin
croaked out all the knowledge that they'd gained.

Oh ancient god of poetry, mortality, and wisdom,
we ask in earshot of our steamroller of progress
that you remind us how those birds brought back
the learning you so craved: a story shaped
by Thought and Memory on the long flight home,
conveyed in raucous caws, and always with an eye
for glimpses of the smash of death below.

Groundwork

In the pre-Viking cemetery archeologists found
the bones of a young woman and next to her,

her stillborn baby tenderly laid upon the wing
of a swan with a small knife knapped from flint

beside its hip. For its journey home, this child
was sent out with a wing and a tool. We could

do no worse as, trembling, we compose
our children for their voyages.

—Vedbæk, Denmark

The Mead of Poetry

In the time-frayed Norse telling,
poetry that sang true came
from drinking an intoxicating mead
first cooked up in kettles by
the terrible brothers, Fjalar and Galar.

To their fermented berry sauce
they added honey and the blood
of the wisest of the gods, Kvasir,
whom they'd lured and killed, thirsty
for the keenness of his eye and ear.

So poetry was stirred up in a vat
of trickery, enticement, wisdom,
spilled blood, sweetness, observation—
substances of the world cooked
down to something new, an alchemy
of recomposing and preserving.

❖

In later chapters of the tale, old Odin,
in an eagle's form, glugged down
his gullet a tankful of this frothy mead,
defiant of the giant bird on guard, then
soared home to share the elixir of true verse
with his fellow gods—and with us,
chased by the furious, screeching giant.

Odin spat up most of the brew
for the word-besotten into his cauldrons,
but a bit slipped out in a foul-smelling fart
that splattered the face of the giant, who could
only sputter, fume, and twitter angry words.

The lesson's clear: beware the honeyed liquor
from an ass. No poetry there.

The Slippage

In bygone Bryggen seaport
unsortable centuries ago,
merchant guild-masters forbade
any fire indoors, even candles,
fearful of quayside infernos
fueled by the salt cod, stockfish,
and rye grain stored to the rafters
in the wharf's wooden warehouses:
pier-packed, chockablock tinder-piles.
So the market men's dealings each day
were done in the dim and the dark.

But fire has its own dire designs.
Decade and decade again,
fanned by fjord-winds and by fish oil
time-seeped into the timber,
devouring flames flared up,
ravaging and razing the waterfront
warren of warehouses, merchant homes,
commerce and quay-clamor and all.

After each time the debris would be dumped,
the conflagration refuse cast
smoldering into the silent sea.
Year by year, layer by layer,
the rubble and wreckage rose,
stretching the shorefront seaward,
the cityscape skyward,
the new town and tenements atop
old trash and trauma,
progress piled up on the ruined.

So, the harbor diminished yet deepened.
Bigger boats could then berth at her docks.

The wharfside goods-markets grew larger,
more fuel for the next famished fire.

Today those old Hansa League holdings
host tourist hordes, history, schlock shops.
Underfoot lie the dregs of the ancestors,
their detritus, their dreams, and their rot.
But scientists measure a slippage,
a decomposition that's constant.

Whatever's burned down can be seedbed.
Whatever's pitched out can provide.
Whatever is ruined can be rebuilt.
The slippage is what will abide.

—Bergen, Norway

IV.

"Some of these things are true and some of them lies.
But they are all good stories."
                              ~ Hilary Mantel, *Wolf Hall*

She Spoke

Where did I hear
that every Japanese poet
was supposed to visit Mt. Fuji
and write a poem?

Basho's was a poem
of absence, something like:

> *Fog-draped day*
> *Can't see Mt. Fuji*
> *Hmm*

Fuji may come from
an old word for *fire master*
and the current kanji
can mean *man of status*

Mt. Fuji mans the horizon
southwest of Tokyo

Northeast of my city, Portland,
we watch Mt. St. Helens

To the Klickitat peoples she was
the beautiful *Loowit*—shapely, serene
between jagged, bickering boyfriends
we call Mounts Hood and Adams

Before 1980, we compared
her to Fuji—snow-clad, quiet,
site for a humble, deferential poem

And then she blew, telling us
with pyroclastic clarity
to heed her power and rage

Loowit's done with silence,
demands a poem of presence:

> *Every day*
> *Loowit speaks on the horizon:*
> *she will be what she wants*

Hmm

The Ingenious Hidalgo

> "To my mind," said Sancho, "there can't be all that many thoughts
> you can use for making up rhymes."
> ~ Cervantes, *Don Quixote*

Well, you can have thoughts of dragons you might slay,
rescue-ready maidens in some perilous plight,
the chance to gallop on your steed into the fray
(home-made lance poised for wrongs to right),
and then standing at the palace balustrades,
new governor of an island kingdom you've been granted,
basking in your subjects' cheers and accolades—
puffed up, beknighted, enchanted.

Such vivid thoughts may be the only power
you have over fate and history and time,
the uncontrollable clanking through the hours
of windmill blades that don't spin to your rhymes.

But sometimes though you're bruised and saddlesore
and disabused of all your boyish dreams,
you clamber back up on your swaybacked horse
and ride off in the light of more moonbeams,
intent on quests and dragons and maidens to caress you—
though armies in the distance prove just baa-ing sheep,
and women are not asking to be rescued,
and dragons have for centuries been asleep.

Still you are riding, seeking, praying,
holding on to your old tilt-for-honor schemes;
meanwhile your best friend's ass won't stop its braying,
so you go home, lie down, and dream more dreams.

The Barflies Discuss the King's Impending Visit

They're buzzing at the Hoodoo Bar & Grill,
the trickster hangout down by Acme Inc.
Rumor has it that the king is on his way.
Robin Goodfellow and John the Conqueroo,
glued to their usual barstools, ponder
a proper gift for the regal flimflam man.
"Blackbirds in a pie would be a dainty dish,"
says John to the chum he calls Puck for short.
"What say, chef?" he yells to old Prometheus,
but that guy's way too busy at the barbecue
on the back deck, cooking up what looks
to be bones wrapped in juicy meat.

Meanwhile Anansi the spider's in the corner
spinning flattery to snare the Con-in-Chief,
and Br'er Rabbit's in the pub's herb garden,
practicing his trusty standby line: "Throw me
anywhere, just not over that wall, man."

In the alley Tom Sawyer inspects his cans
of whitewash, getting ready for the king's
broad brushwork. Good Soldier Schweik
sits in a booth, practicing his slag-off salute.

Reynard the Fox and Coyote rack the balls
at the pool table in the back room, pull their
red hats over their ears, set up the scam.
"So easy to hustle a hustler," says Rey.

Oona McCool, proprietor of the joint,
just shakes her head and sighs, "Boys, boys,
boys." And quietly bakes another fry pan
into her fourteenth loaf of royal griddle bread.

Starlings and the Bard

Shakespeare knew his birds.
They swarm the pages
of his plays and poems:
> "the crows and choughs
> that wing the midway air"
> in *Lear,*   in *Winter's Tale*
>   "the lark that tirra-lirra chants,"
and more: the ready metaphors
of doves,
     cocks,
          eagles,
               vultures,
but also rarer flocks of buntings,
     daws, rooks, cormorants,
          and   squawking popinjays.

Decades ago some foolish snipe,
an avid ornithologist, decided
to import to Central Park
all the birds he found perched
on lines of Shakespeare's works.
And so in winter 1890 this mad loon
let loose his first feathery fleet,
     a chattering of sixty starlings
into the frigid New York air,
     and forty more the next year.

     These muscled little birds, prolific breeders,   took
     to the sky of their new homeland, winging   west.
     In a century   they'd spread   across the country
     coast   to   coast,
       two hundred million at last count—a noisy,
       vast affliction of these gangsters of the air
         in their metallic coats   with
            shiny   studs.

See, starlings nest in tree-holes, but
vacancies are hard to come by.
So mimicking others'
calls, these brutes
invaded, sneaked into
the nests that other birds
had built, peck-whacked
all eggs, evicted the gentler residents.
Pugnacious squatters with no scruples,
these birds became notorious avian Mafiosi.

Ah, Will, what would your ink-quill make
of these feathered bullets of the firmament,
bad-ass bruisers of the roost, birdyard bullies
loosed into the air, and all because of cuckoo
dreams of honoring you? What would you say
above the racket of a starling murmuration?

Perhaps:
    Be wary of the way that stirring words
    can lead to tyrants preening on a perch.

After Act V

The stage descends to black

and in that momentary suspension
in the dark and silent theater,
we inhale in quiet the grief and pity.

And then the lights come up, we blink,
and in the glare, we're battered
into everydayness once again. Hamlet,
Gertrude, Claudius, and Laertes have leapt
from their deathbeds, are upright and smiling,
holding hands, bowing from the waist. The crowd
erupts, standing, clapping in a frenzy. Horatio laughs,
basking in acclaim. Ophelia scans the room
for her new boyfriend who's come to see the play
for the first time. Hamlet's all puffed up, his pride
palpable. They take four bows amid huzzahs,
then leave the stage lifeless, strewn with swords,
an empty stoup of wine, a forlorn crown,
and gouts of blood.

We are expected to check our cellphones,
scoop up scarves and jackets, slowly
sardine down the aisle, shamble through
the lobby, exit left, our minds on other matters:
getting to the car, which route to take home,
cash for the sitter, sweat about tomorrow's
obligations and the thousand tiny slings
and arrows of the daily shuffle.

But I don't want to move, don't want
the lights up, can't so quickly hit that switch.
Please leave us longer in this darkness
that o'er-crows our spirits, absent us

from felicity awhile, from comfort
and evasion. Let us steep in sadness,
ache for wisdom, feel in empty silence
all the sorrows of all our plays.
Oh, friends, don't clap, don't go away.
This isn't where the story ends.

A Peaceful Uproar

We finish our meal with a hotchpotch soup of poems on history, parenthood, family, teaching, friendship.

Or maybe a better metaphor for this section comes from the old stone soup folktale: A stranger comes to a town with a cooking pot that he fills with water, plops a stone into, and sets atop a fire he's built. He takes a spoon from his patchwork coat and starts stirring. Curious villagers come by, wondering about this soup, which the traveler offers to share. However, he says as he samples a spoonful, it seems something is slightly off, some subtle taste missing. One villager, anticipating a bowlful, says maybe it needs a potato for body and runs home to snag a spud from the bin to add to the pot. Another villager tosses in a pinch of salt, another a handful of carrots, another some turnips, another a sprig of rosemary. Soon all the townsfolk have added their contributions, and a tasty soup is enjoyed by all.

Throw your own spices in here.

I.

"Rise free from care before the dawn
and seek new adventures."
~ H.D. Thoreau,
Walden, or Life in the Woods

Up Eagle Creek Trail

Streamside's mild amble
climbs quickly to cliff-side, walls
towering skyward.

I hang to the line,
grasping rock-anchored cables
along the steep path.

At one-point-five miles,
Metlako Falls Overlook
Spur Trail slants creekward.

At two miles in, there's
riverfall rumble below.
Mist sprinkles my face.

I choose this way down,
drop to the pool just below
the Punch Bowl Falls din.

Above there's a shout,
and leaping through green air, a
man drops, legs cycling.

He splats in the pool
and surfaces, sputtering.
His friends laugh above.

Scores of flags flutter:
fern fronds ruffling in the wind,
clinging to cliffwalls.

The creek loudly pours,
runs pounding and rocketing
away, downhill bound.

Full-throated creeksong
lifts along the canyonsides,
a peaceful uproar.

II.

"...people are trapped in history and
history is trapped in them."
~ James Baldwin,
"Stranger in the Village"

History

a few miles south of Drain, Oregon

Once or twice a year on the drive south
to see our boys and their sweet crews

we catch a fly-by glimpse of a swaybacked barn
sinking slowly, month by month, earth-drawn

by its weight of beam, rotting plank and memory,
settling as we once again whoosh by, reminder

of the long decline of what we make and do not
tend. A bulldozer would be a mercy. Knock it down,

I think. Show some respect. Don't leave this old
skeleton naked, exposed, beat down. One year

we saw some vandal had emptied a spraycan
on the spavined barn, a slash of paint

in neon green that spelled out "HISTORY,"
a shout-out to termites, fungi, worms.

We roar past HISTORY and ponder for a blink
this one-time worksite, home for animals,

shelter for tools—and the fleeting glimpse of words
that sing a dirge of woodrot, rain, wind, time,

and gravity. And carelessness. The AC hums. Carefree,
we drive. Road to gobble, miles to go, HISTORY to flee.

Geneva, Nebraska

On our trip back to her hometown
west of Omaha, in a flat stretch of farmland,
we walk to the town square with its bandstand
and vast lawn around the county courthouse.
My mother remembers eating watermelon at the curb
with her friend, as the town band played on Fourth of July,
and looking across the street to her dad's Ford agency,
and hoping she might see her mother puttering by
in the family sedan, one of the few women in town
who could drive, and always in her fancy hats.
My mom closes her eyes at the pleasure of
spitting seeds into the gutter.

Their house was on a corner of H Street, big enough
for three kids and an extra room to rent to the schoolteacher.
The Methodist Church, where her father directed the choir,
was down the street. Not many folks had a phone.
Their number was 1-3, my mother recalls.

But Black Tuesday came, the Crash, and 1930.
Car sales dried up, and Ford closed the agency.
Her parents had to sell the house—last one they ever owned—
and move to Omaha. My grandfather sold insurance
for Cosmopolitan Life, until it went under,
and another company whose name she can't remember,
until it, too, went bust. That summer my mom was sent
to Falls City south of Omaha to live with relatives,
and when she came home all the furniture had been sold
and there was a new rental place to stay in,
and later another, and another, and another.
For a couple of years, an aunt and cousin moved in,
Uncle Huey lost to the drink, and another year
my mom and her brother lived in the basement
of the hill house of rich kin, while her mother was bed-sick.

Her father pitched rug-cleaning services door-to-door
until that outfit failed, but finally got steady work
selling gravestones for Uncle Al's monument shop,
death a Depression-proof client.

"That must've been hard," I say, listening to those stories again.
My mom spits that seed into the gutter.
"We weren't poor," she tells me, looking at the photos I took
of the grand old house on H Street, now needing paint.
"We were never poor."

A Minnesota Boy
Drafted and Sent for Basic Training
to Ft. McArthur
in San Pedro, California, 1942

He'd brought his ice skates
out from home, took the bus
to Long Beach to see
Sonja Heinie's Ice Palace—
in a tent!

"She was something," he said.
"And I wouldn't have ever believed
I could skate in my shirtsleeves."

Now since he brought a bullet home
from the freezing beach at Gold,
he's lived in Long Beach,
takes the bus downtown—
night man at the warehouse
in his shirtsleeves
even on the coolest nights.

"She was something, man."

The Janitor

Sarge, thick and blue-faced,
slowly mopped the school halls,
swimming in his dreams.
"I was in WW II, son," he said
over his bucket, "the Big One."
He led his scared platoon,
just kids fresh out of high school,
through snow and Jerry bullets
in the winter of the Bulge—
snow thick as salmon runs
back home in Oregon, he said,
the way they used to be.
He had to be hard, he said,
to save his boys.

In snow-white overalls old Sarge,
crew-cutted still and stern,
mopped the floors in winter,
emptied trashcans for the kids.
They'd laugh when he would bark at them
to quit their writing on the walls.
Hard to save his boys.

One day he flopped down in the hall
and knocked himself against the deck.
His heart fanned fast and stopped.
We fished him from the snow.

A Child's Guide to Difficult
But Useful Words: 1950's Edition

1. *Mercurochrome*:
    medicine painted with a glass tube
    on your skinned-up knees and elbows,
    the cherry-red slash atop the scrape
    a mark of honor.

2. *Honor*

3. *Onomatopoeia*:
    what Miss Ruz told you about
    in third grade:
    bam crash zoom bang whizz.
    "How about piss?" someone whispered—
    maybe you.

4. *Narthex and nave*:
    dark places where you hear
    about trespasses more tricky
    on the tongue and mortal soul
    than your everyday *bad* or *lazy*.
    But also *sanctuary*.

5. *Flathead, Phllips head, clutchhead, hex*:
    tools you have to put back
    carefully in the right place
    on the pegboard behind the workbench.

6. *Juvenile delinquent*:
    what your teachers and the minister
    warn about—
    maybe you.

7. *Mortuary, coffin, interment*:
   where your grandparents disappeared.
   And *repose*.

8. *Carburetor, alternator, generator, crankshaft, transmission*:
   the secret language of your older brother
   and your dad.

9. *Polio, tuberculosis, leukemia, lockjaw*:
   shadows that pass over
   careless children—
   maybe you.

The Choice

Caryl Chessman dies in the San Quentin
gas chamber, May 1960

The two pills break
the water in the bucket
with a sput rehearsed
for months, heard in the flush
of every crummy seatless toilet,
a deathly tune in every
clunk of mop and bucket
slow-dancing up the block
between the cells.

Official witnesses recount
this much: that you,
the bound condemned,
you held your breath.
Your face filled up with blood.
You hugged to anaerobic life,
you counted searing seconds
spinning by as you filled up
with toxins in your lungs
till forced to finally suck
the blistering air.

A trade: two minutes of
your fiercest struggle,
arched in agony for air,
for seconds of assent
to numbing fact.

The choice that you were cut:
concede to life's last moment's
sour smell or suffer as
you drown in your desire.

Czechoslovakia: July 20, 1969
one year after the invasion

Remind me again
of that train
in the night
and the rain
of bright sparks
screaming by
in the dark

and the hostel
in old Prague
when we watched
the moon landing
on the lobby TV
with the crowd
of young Czechs
who raised cheers
for the Yanks and
their poke in the eye
of the Russians
who'd crowed that
they'd get there first
while dark-coated
soldiers sullenly stood
their Warsaw Pact watch
on street corners outside

On that trip we
found friendship
that later turned love
and the hard rub
of history to help us
remember through
all our long years

that dark troops
lurk mutely
around many corners

So remind me
of the dark
on the night line
from Prague
and those sparks
in the air

Serpents and Daggers

Lyrics to a song by the band Big Blind
written for a neighbor boy killed at 21
by a land mine in Iraq, July 2003

He was an itchy-foot kid from the neighborhood,
Free-spirit, joker, mostly doing what he should,
A bagboy at the grocery store to earn himself a dime.
For him on most days school just seemed a waste of time.
He was searching for direction, the parish priest said,
But don't put a halo on this boy's head.

He drove his mama crazy but she loved him to the bone,
Raising him and his little brother all alone,
This punk rock drummer in raggedy jeans.
Then one day he signed himself up with the U.S. Marines.

He had a few months before his hair'd get chopped.
He started going down to the tattoo shop,
Got serpents up his arms and daggers on his chest.
"Not another one," his mama said. "You give me no rest."
But even when she pleaded with him, "Boy, you cut it out,"
One day he had a new scab across his back to brag about.
He peeled off the bandage to show his new tat:
"Mom" was inked in ornate script, and that, she knew, was that.
"It just seemed right," he joked, "since you're always on my back."
She laughed and wept and hugged him till the night turned black.

Those weeks she couldn't let him go, she'd cry and hold him tight,
But had to put him on a Greyhound bus late one night.
Once in Iraq he volunteered for a landmine-clearing crew,
Wrote to his uncle about the things he had to do.
He couldn't tell his mom, he said, she'd just fret and weep.
But honor, Uncle Johnny, is a word we're selling cheap.

Now the lesson is a serpent that coils up our arm.
We better know the truth of words that send kids into harm.
He was just another boy from a neighborhood,
Desperate for once to do something good.

I dream of daggers flying through a desert night
And a kid who just wanted to make things right.
Now the priest looks down upon that mom dressed up in black.
That boy's name is carved forever across all our backs.

I Can't Breathe

for Eric Garner, d. July 17, 2014

A black man selling smokes
is bulldogged to the ground.
Restraint by neck compression
killed the man, the coroner found.

An old white man writes poems
alone at his quiet desk.
His world unfolds in stanzas
of restraint: life compressed.

The poet's grandson is black.
This world has hard truths words must face.
Poems can bear our deepest blues, but Lord
what poem can keep that young man safe?

Citizens United

If money can be speech

Why can't
  trees be bank accounts
  salmon runs the GDP
  and birdsong our full-throated patriotism?

Let's declare
  wildflower beds our stock market
  forest breaks our border-crossing stations
  lichen-crusted stones our dearest principles
  rivers our Congress in session
  redwood groves our "world's greatest deliberative body"
  children the First Amendment
  grandchildren the Second
  and coral reefs our Bill of Rights.

If we can make such magic
  transformations with a simple gavel-smack
  then let's decree:
  in our Supreme Court
  the stars overhead will be our last appeal.

III.

"... it's a solid lesson in the limitations of self
to realize your heart is running around inside
someone else's body."
~ Christopher Hitchens,
Hitch-22: A Memoir

Fractions

"What's bigger?" asked my big brother,
beginning another conclusive proof of things
I needed to be reminded I was ignorant about.
He pointed at the figures he'd written—
1/8 and 1/5. Even in kindergarten I knew
my numbers, so I pointed to the one with the eight.
"That's bigger." "No, you're wrong," he said.
"That's a fraction. It's the smaller one." I,
the smaller one, balked in incomprehension. And
by the time I got to fractions and did finally get it,
he was on to decimals and other bafflements.

"You think you can pour all the water
out of a soda bottle faster than me?" asked
my big brother in the kitchen. Two empties,
the green-tinted glass catching the Saturday
morning light, sat on the counter. "Let's see,"
I said, always a game mark for a challenge.
We both filled our bottles with tap water,
then stood side by side at the sink. I figured
somehow he had the advantage being taller,
but I was determined to turn my bottle
upside down so fast he'd finally lose. "Go,"
he said. And as the water blubbed out
of my inverted bottle, he took a second
to swirl his, and that liquid whirlpooled
out of his bottle's mouth and down the drain
along with my hope, faster than the course
of my perplexity. "It's physics, little bro,"
he said, "just simple physics."

Sixty years later, and little bro is still
trying to prove himself—with the slow
splash of a poem, perhaps—but those

old stories swirl quickly down the drain.
Brotherhood has its hard-to-fathom fractions:
love can appear confoundingly small,
but it's bigger than you think.

Two-Year-Old Shirtless in the Garden,
Tanned and Face Smeared with Blackberry Juice

My son
turned dark
this summer
in the sun.
He's wild now,
wild and sweet
and young.
The pruning
happens soon
enough.

Reading with a Son

Pooh Bear and Piglet
went after a Woozle
in *Pooh* Chapter Three.
The story's a doozy:
the footprint's a puzzle,
and Pooh's all a-muddle,
the mystery's not easy.
Encircled, Pooh's dizzy.

My son said, "A Woozle?
Is that true or not?
I thought it was weasel."
Well, who wants to quibble?
"I think so," I said.
That was that.

Croup

The dry cough
woke us, the small cry
for help. In the dark
she got the advice nurse
on the phone.
I carried our son—
limp, sick, barking—
downstairs,
flipped on the bathroom light,
clicked off the fan,
closed the door.
With one hand I turned
the hot water on, full blast.
Steam filled the room,
vapor of our hope.
I sat on the edge of the tub,
my son in my arms
struggling to breathe,
so light, so trusting,
as if I really knew what to do
to help him.
I feel the surrender still in my arms,
the small loosening of muscle and trust;
he looked at me so afraid but grateful
for what he thought I knew.
We sweated through it together.

I still feel that weight tonight
on the phone line—
that boy taller than I am now—
and I think
I wish I could hold you,
but I still don't know how
to help you breathe.

The vapor of my fear
fills the room.
May we sweat this one out, too.
Breathe, son, please.

A Christmas Song After Listening to a Children's Choir

May our children lift our world-weighed hearts
With their voices soaring to the stars,
And as we listen drop us to our knees
To live up to our words of peace that they believe.

Leaks in the Attic

A damp spot on the living room ceiling
and a small blister of paint compel me
to the attic crawl space. Seems rain
is quietly invading my home.

"Water finds its own way," my buddy
the builder had said when I'd shared my worry.
"It'll seep in slowly and surprise you.
Damn hard to figure where it comes from.
Keep looking around."

On my knees under the long slope
of roofline, I push aside old boxes, taped
and labeled: "Boys' books," "Blocks,"
"Nate Trains," and "Josh Matchbox Cars."
They're dry. I creep to the far end where the leak
might be, peel away the insulation, run
my fingers down the join of joist and roofboard,
mindful of nails, feeling for dampness or rot.
Dry there. I keep looking around. Finally,
at the back corner, I find the spot, a tiny vein
of moistness, the place to fix.

Backing out, knee-sore, I move the boxes
back where they were, the old toys and gear
we cannot bring ourselves to give up. Our sons
have found their own way.
Under the long slope of time,
the insulation peels away.
There's another leak.

A Father's Promise
to his sons

Boys,
if a veil falls
over my eyes,
I will always see you.
If a curtain drops
over my mind,
I will always know you.
If I can no longer hear,
I will always recognize
your voices.
If I leave faster
than anyone expects—
the heart blown up,
the plummeting airplane—
you will be my last
brave happy thought.
If I leave slower
than anyone expects,
you will be my last
brief cogent thought.
No matter.
When I go,
I will never leave you.

Leaf-Fall

The late fall day is clear and cold;
the wind stirs.
The mottled leaves are letting go.

In their descent through air
there's no straight line:
gust-buffeted, they're blown
and tumbled, twirled, twined.

Resistant to earth's pull,
they pause to shiver, float,
and with the next puff rush
away, whirl till the wind slows,
and finally settle, choiceless,
to the soggy ground below.

I slowly do an old man's dance,
a shiver in my bones,
leaf-season jig my small resistance:
I can't—not yet—let go.

IV.

"Was I gleeful, settled, content, during the hours I passed
in yonder bare, humble schoolroom...?"

~ Charlotte Brontë, *Jane Eyre*

A Hesitant Love Poem
to second period English class on the occasion of Valentine's Day

Now listen up, class.
I know this is hard to hear.

See, I remember the shock of spotting Miss Duryee
pushing her cart at the grocery store
past the oranges, mounded high,
and her saying hello
and chatting calmly with my mother
as I stared dumbfounded
at my first grade teacher
out in the world.

Now, I loved Miss Duryee
and learning to read at her orderly tables,
coloring within careful boundaries,
finding out what a paragraph was
and how vowels said their letter names
but had secret names, too,
and the magic of lining up sums.

But this sighting in the grocery store
did not line up.
Why was she *there*?
Miss Duryee had her world
where Bluebirds sat at one table
and Robins at another,
where paste and paint had
their own cubbyholes,
where paragraphs were clearly indented.
This store, though, was not her place,
but full of disorder:
potatoes piled drunkenly in bins,
grapes squashed on the linoleum floor,

and people in crooked check-out lines
like my mom and me.
I loved Miss Duryee,
but love has its careful boundaries.

So it's hard for me to figure out how to tell you
how much I feel for you on this Valentine's Day.
Things have their places and secret names.

A bluebird squawks
outside the classroom window.

The oranges were bright
and stacked to the sky.

Ode to My Student's Pen

She is perched
on the ledge of his shirt pocket
like a small parrot.
Her plump green torso
tenses in his hand
when he takes her from his pocket
for exercise or tricks.
May she resist this business
with the small insistent
flutter of her wildness.

Teacher as King Kong

The beast, huge in his hair suit,
leapt like a ballerina
into the air.
Lightly he pirouetted
on two students' bodies,
Freddy and Erika,
now flat and slippery as
old banana peel.
His entrechat
knocked six students senseless:
Monica, Billy Bob, Sue, Kym, Bud, Shakur.
The back table screamed
as he did a nimble turn
up on his toes
crushing four more of them,
none identifiable,
knocking the chalkboards
clean off the walls.
Finally he bowed to
a strange absence of applause.

For the Group Under the Table

That day, I'd scattered the class into groups
to discuss the pages they'd been assigned to read
the night before in Achebe's *Things Fall Apart*.
I circled the room to eavesdrop, kibitz, encourage;
stopped at one table to answer a question, another to pose one,
sat at a third to exult in the insight of a normally quiet boy.
When I stood, though, something seemed missing.
I soon saw: the group in the back corner had vanished—
Amanda and Christine, Shannah and Carolyn.
My head on a swivel, I started a search mission,
but the mystery proved easy to solve.
Those four had decided to meet *under* their table.
Circled together on the old rug of the classroom,
backs curved, cross-legged, knees touching,
huddled up with their books in their hands,
they were earnestly sharing whatever they'd found
in that spare and disquieting book.

I knelt down to join them, awkward in size and age,
and thought, *I can't get down under there.*
They're flexible; I'm not. Plus it's not my place.
So I threw my voice from above: "How's it going down there?"
"Great," one quickly answered. Another needed to explain:
"It's less noisy down here, Mr. G. We can concentrate."
Stiffly, I rose, and left the group under the table
discussing the story, its hero's hard heart, the mystery
of all hearts, themselves—hunkered down where a teacher can't go.
I wandered the room, stopping and stirring, provoking the others,
but wondering about those four who'd disappeared.
Why am I worried? I thought. *Things are not falling apart.*
They're not lost.

They'd left the world of the stiff somewhere up above:
they were shouldered around a fire, talking through the dark;
down in a storm cellar, singing the tempest away;

clumped in a molehole, nibbling sweet roots;
sailing in steerage across unseen seas;
downstairs in a den sharing slumber party secrets;
digging with picks at the veins in a silver mine;
underground at a jazz club, inventing new riffs;
at a gathering in a think tank, dizzy with theories;
piled in a root dugout, sprouting;
in an underground card club, taking a chance;
in a dank basement studio, swaying to music,
      lost in the dancer and dance.

Save

The chalkboard is covered with messages:
   Lit Log for Thursday: Your definition of comedy
   Read to Act III in The Importance of Being Earnest
   Sign up for conferences
   Fri: Projects due

I have classes over a two-day schedule, and I don't want to write the same things again and again on the chalkboard. I want some messages to last longer than this day. So I chalk a note for the custodian, Dan, who will otherwise erase it all. "Save," I write next to what I want saved, and circle it.

I scan the chalkboard, deciding what to save.

Save this schedule, this assignment, this notice, this standard, these words.

Save the questions that sustain us.

Save the memory of Mitchell's challenges and Janie's laughter.

Save the daily facts of Angel's confusion and Zack's jokes, Ephraim's silence and Ronni's enthusiasm.

Save the patient desire that turns Jarren brilliant in spite of his learning disability.

Save today's miraculous story by Leeza, usually stoned and angry, of her grandmother's hunger in Poland during World War II. Save for us all the chance to see Leeza in new ways.

Save today's frustrated note from Chloe, who wrote, "You didn't understand me at all, Mr. G., or what I was saying." Save the hope of trying again.

Save the lingering sound of Marissa and Shannon singing in two-part harmony before second period started today. Save their song and their moxie and the possibility of joy.

Save the empty seat of Jacob, who left. Dropped out. Nobody took his chair.

Save Caitlin's exultation: "I nailed it, Mr. G!"

Save me from cynicism and habit.

Save Antoine's muttering, "Screw this comedy shit." Save him from knowing I heard.

Save him. Save me.

Save.

Lit Teacher

Day after day I'm up there pitching tales
they read or don't, ignore or embrace
like hopefuls at the eighth grade dance.
Some drop anchors, some set sails.

One girl says she finds herself on the page
of a dusty play about kings and ghosts.
One boy protests. He says, "These are just
made-up people for pretending on a stage."

She clears her throat, has more to quietly say:
"No, I love that nunnery girl. She knows my story.
She's real, alone. She speaks, but then she's sorry."
The boy just snorts. The girl is brave but looks away,

because the saying of her love is a lonely thing.

with apologies for poaching
from William Stafford's "Lit Instructor"

Senior English, Late May

getting close to Commencement

Outside my classroom window
I watch a clump of trees:
big-leafed maple,
hawthorn, hazelnut—
new-bloomed, spring-green,
sap-rich, seeds ready
to ride the next wind.

Against the wall,
one well-rooted Doug fir,
brown at its needle tips,
won't let go its cones yet.

I turn back to my students.
"Okay," I say, "let's get started.
We only have three weeks left
and so much still to cover."
I feel unprepared.
The class is ready.
The wind stirs.

V.

"I count myself in nothing else so happy
As in a soul remembering my good friends."
~ William Shakespeare,
Richard II

Bucking Hay for Pat

at Lochinvar Farm, Banks, Oregon

Del gone earlier that year, Pat's knee bum,
she needs help to get the hay up in her barn.
She could hire it out, but asks three long-time pals,
cityboys past our prime, to drive out from Portland
to Banks for the use of our old muscles and friendship.
"Bring heavy gloves," she'd said, "and beat-up jeans
and long-sleeved shirts. I'll have the beer cold."
We cross the urban line into the swaybacked farmland
of Tualatin Valley, Mt. Hood a sentinel behind us.
The sun's out, the October air cool and ripening into fall.

Pat waits at the barn. Her grown son Ty, sweet as cut grass,
has already brought the first load back on the flatbed.
He eyes his greybeard crew, gives a quick lesson in bucking:
"Use, don't fight, the bale-weight. It's all legs, knee, momentum.
Save your backs, boys, and watch your feet. On the truck,
it's easy to slip between bales; we don't need any bones snapped."

We pull on our gloves, start loading. Off the truck, into the barn.
The first rows are easy and we catch the rhythm
in the lift and stack. Slowly the scratchy fifty-pound bales
climb the back wall of the barn, its air thick
with haydust, sun through the cracks, sneezing.

Four times into the long light of the autumn afternoon,
we drive down Harrington Road, past the old grade school,
reload the ancient flatbed, chug back to Pat's place,
stack bales toward the rafters. Soon it's all sweat and jokes,
grunt and itch and *oof*, aching arms and aching knees.
No bones snap. The pace declines, but still we buck.
Finally, at dusk, the barn's piled high, the job done.

Pat builds a bonfire. We sit around in lawn chairs,
warmed by the crackle and chat, drying out,
alfalfa chaff in every junction of collar and neck,
sleeve and wrist, sock and ankle. The ponies nose the field.
Mt. Hood's alight in alpenglow. We drink, stack high
our plates with sausages, Pat's potato salad, stories.
We laugh and talk of the day, of Del, of our momentum
and our decline, of slips, the grunt and glory of the work,
the itch of friendship that sticks under our sweat-dried shirts.

The Sailor on His Front Porch

My pal Ben
talks with his hands.
We're on his front porch,
shooting the breeze,
but he's still on his boat last week,
back in the race, describing
the Cape, the chop, the fetch
of wind-swept water, showing me
with a sawtoothing hand
the tack and beat to windward.
On his porch, Ben mans
the sheet again, hears
his helmsman yell, feels
the sail slacken.

Landsman to my marrowbone,
I don't know this lingo—heading up,
running close to the wind—
but Ben at the sheet
trims and fills my sails.
Our wives are ready
for us to come ashore,
but on his front porch,
Ben's back on his boat,
water-bound, bearing away,
lost to the shift of the sea.
I'm lost in his hands.

to Ben Smith
and the Blind Sailing Regattas

Big Blind at the Bay Haven

The band gets a gig at the Bay Haven Inn,
the fisherman's bar on the lee side of Newport
next door to the first Mo's, where the chowder
is creamy, the fish fresh off the boat.

The Fat Tire beer sign stutters in neon.
Est. 1908, it blinks. *Think about it, boys,*
Andrew says, *we're playing a joint*
with a century of sweat soaked into the walls,
and salt air and fishscales and fish tales.

Inside we set up—drum kit, keyboard, bass man,
lead and rhythm axes, and me with my harp case,
gleaming tin sandwiches lined up in a row—then
run through a warm-up, tape set lists to the floor.

Ten minutes till you start, guys, the barkeep says.
It's ten to nine. *Have a brew on us, look around.*
Above walls crammed with photos of old boats
with their catches and crews, a brace of deer heads
keeps watch, staring blankly at some shoreline.
An hombre in back at the pool table racks the balls
with a clatter. The barkeep pulls me an ale
from the Fat Tire tap, and right before showtime
we all hike to the head to pump bilges.

The joint starts to fill, and it's time to go on.
We step to the stage, gear up, take that last sip,
give Andrew a nod, and he counts us in.
With a crash of Stick's snare, we're launched:
Gypsy woman told my momma, before I was born
You got a boy-child comin', gonna be a son-of-a-gun...

Twelve bars in, we're in the pocket. Joel's thumb is
thumping the bass. The barflies, barmaids, and
burger bangers swivel to watch. *Everybody
knows I'm here*, crows Andrew at the turn.

First set lasts an hour and change. Outside
on break, we lean against the Bay Haven wall.
A banner above says *Big Blind: Tonite!* and Mikey
is checking out the tourist girls who crowd
the summer streets. *Yeah, ladies, Big Blind,
that's us. What, no one wants an autograph?*

Johnny came up with that name playing poker.
In hold'em, the big blind's a pre-flop bet,
your statement: here's what I'll throw down
before a single card is dealt, my wager that I'll
be lucky in contradiction to all the evidence
of my life, but here I am anyway, chips stacked
at the table, willing and ready. Slap 'em down.

I look out the street to the leaping curves
of Yaquina Bay Bridge, past the spars all atilt:
the fishing fleet at anchor in the deepening night,
the masthead lights swaying there on the swells.
The music of the day is still stuck to the street—
cannery clank and seagull screech, sea lion honk,
the barkers' unspooling spiels at Ripley's Believe It
or Not, the summertime hubbub of hankering and hope
from the chattering crowds on the walkway.

The din of the crowd and clinking of glasses drags us
back in. Now the joint's packed, ready for the second set.
We step up to the stage, eyes on the horizon, looking for
that launching spot, that fish that slipped the line,

that perfect girl for Mike, that bet on *believe it* rather
than *not*, that big blind hit, that promise of aces
we might always be dealt. Andrew, man,
count us in.

What's Left

Dave calls from across the years
his voice still that husky
roar of smoke and time

Forty years ago we rode together
knights errant tilting at
the windmills of our youth

We smoked and drank our way
through Cold War, hot wars
the roar and discord of the world
and decided all the signs were ripe
the world was coming to an end
and Walter Cronkite would
sign us off

So what's left when
you've done your time marching
talking, writing letters, petitioning
and it's not enough

At the end of the teetering universe
we drank a beer to friendship
and its imminent extinguishing
sitting on a porch above Portola Valley
looking out across the scrub oaks
through the smoke of distant fires

The sun went down
Walter Cronkite signed off
the world didn't end
and we could not see
through the smoke
what would be left
when we'd made our lives

Worlds have been smothered
and relighted since that night
and when the world goes poof
once more, Dave, I'd like to be
on that porch again with you

But now we talk from miles away
about grandkids
and drinking too much
and lost packages
and the fragile states of our hearts

The windmills, still stretching
to the roaring sea,
clank on, and our old plugs
complain about our weight

VI.

"When we try to pick out anything by itself,
we find it hitched to everything else in the universe."
~ John Muir, *My First Summer in the Sierra*

Separations

Home late from work
on a dry winter Wednesday,
kick off my shoes
then remember that midweek chore,
in my socks start the separating:
      Glass in yellow tub
      Recyclables in blue cart
      Compost and yard debris in green
      Trash for the landfill in brown

Night is half-fallen,
east wind sweeps the driveway
when I roll out the carts,
too tired to put back on my shoes,
position the carts on the street
for the parade of trash trucks
that will roar through in the morning

At the curb, I look up,
see perched on the roofline
a thin slice of moon, horns up
in a luminous beaming and the rest
of the earth-shadowed moon face
black against the purpling sky

This: house peak, moon phase, star shimmer,
night curtain in slow free-fall
and a cockeyed lunar grin
smirking at our separations:
      Beauty in the bruised sky
      Trash lined up on the street
      Me in my old socks

Do You Ever

"Do you ever have that feeling,"
he asked, hesitantly,
"of a second head floating up
away from your head
and kind of displacing itself
about a foot above and to the side,
so you've got like this second head
sort of floating there,
and as you're doing something,
whatever you're doing,
you're simultaneously watching
yourself doing that thing,
observing yourself acting
as you're acting, as if
you were both the player
and the director in a booth up there
thinking about how it's going
as you're following the action
on the opening night of the play,
the play that will run
just one performance,
and you know you're the one
who can determine everything
about the role, and you're also the one
who has no control whatsoever
but the deepest critical interest
in how it will all turn out, this scene,
and you're sympathetic to
that poor schlub down there
all alone on the stage, hoping
he doesn't screw everything up,
but at the same time, you're wishing
you were the cold-hearted dude

calmly assessing everything
floating above it all up there?"

She eyed him warily,
watching herself.
"No," she said.

Saving Time

That Sunday morning
when the time change came,
I zig-zagged the house
switching time forward,
rotating hands on the analog clocks
with a finger, holding down
buttons on the digitals as
the red numbers flashed ahead.
Now the days get longer, lighter.

The newsman last night
gave us all a tut-tut:
"It's daylight *saving* time,"
he said, "not *savings*."

That spun me back in time
to the speech I gave from notecards
in seventh grade Current Events,
my topic the Cold War and the old fools
with fingers on the buttons, but Mr. Stoa
stopped time when he interrupted
and corrected me, "It's not *nuke-YOU-lure*,"
he said, "it's *nu-CLEE-urr*." I flashed red,
upset at my teacher's confusion
between the forms and the facts.

In every season we're spinning,
either toward some greater light
or a long incoming darkness.

Some Things I Don't Know
"We're all ignorant, just about different things."
    ~ Will Rogers

The names of sweeps of trees
The name of that rust-breasted bird
That tip-of-the-tongue, um...
Limitless words, words, words

Anything about opera or lepidoptery
    (beyond their smack of beauty)

How to use a slide rule
How to use an abacus
How to use the periodic table
    (and knowing its significance)
How to distinguish stratus, cirrus, cumulus

Anything about Dante or Proust
    (hard confession for this teacher of lit)
How not to bloviate when I know things
When I don't, how to admit it
And the difference

Why Shakespeare wrote in iambic pentameter
And why I still succumb to that dumb metronome
And who reads tabloids at the market checkout stand
And why I can't recall that guy by the orange bin's name

Anything these days
about the workings under the hood of my car

How to bare scars
Where rage comes from
When to be righteously angry at injustice
How to find equilibrium

Anything about astrophysics
    (beyond gaping at the starry sky in wonder)

Much about hunger
Much about wine
Much about most everything

The next line

Notes
on a Few of the Poems

What Shall I Sing?—page 53

The first published poet of Old English whose name we know was an illiterate stable-tender named Cædmon who labored at a 7th-Century monastery overlooking the North Sea in Yorkshire. According to the account by the venerable Anglo-Saxon historian Bede, this Cædmon had poems and songs in his heart, but when the monks started singing and playing the harp at feast times, Cædmon would leave to go sleep with his animals in the barn, shamed by his ignorance of the rules of music and verse. One night, says Bede, an angel appeared to Cædmon in a dream and told him he had a responsibility to share his gift. Out of his shyness and lack of confidence, his anguished reply was, "What shall I sing?" *Everything*, the angelic muse told him. Everything. Just start from the beginning.

The Old Men of Argos—page 57

In *Agamemnon*, the tragedy written some 2,500 years ago by the Athenian playwright Aeschylus, the Chorus consists of men from the city-state of Argos too old to join warriors sailing off to fight in the Trojan War. In the 1962 Paul Roche translation, the Choristers lament being left behind but chant their consolation: "Their saga at least I can sing/For even senility still/Can draw on the breath of the gods/To cast a spell with song."

Trojan Horse with Orange Mane—page 60

In Greek mythology, Epeius was the architect of the fabled wooden horse of the Trojan War. He not only built the thing, he was one of the warriors hiding when the Trojans pulled it inside their gated city.

Cassandra in Three Acts—page 61

The line "You can do anything when you're a star" comes from the infamous Access Hollywood tape. Check it out online.

Attic Ads—page 63

In this bit of tomfoolery, "Attic" in the title is used in its old sense as a reference to ancient Athens, since these advertisements all use in their pitches celebrity endorsements from Greek mythical characters. For the full effect, you might re-read the wonderful old tales of Procrustes, Tantalus, Arachne, Icarus, Phaeton, and Pandora.

She Spoke—page 77

In the lore of the indigenous Klickitat people of the area near where Portland, Oregon, was later settled, the chief of all gods had two sons, Pahto (who lived to the north of what we now call the Columbia River) and Wy'east (who lived to the south). Their territories were joined by a land bridge over the river. Sadly, both boys fell in love with the same young woman, Loowit, who could not choose between them. Their quarrel over her was so violent it shook down the Bridge of the Gods, creating the great cascades of the Columbia River Gorge, including Celilo Falls where tribes from up and down the river gathered for thousands of years to fish and trade. To stop the melee, the chief of the gods struck down his boys and Loowit and transformed them into the three mountains that grace our horizon. Wy'east, with his head pridefully lifted, became what we call Mount Hood, located in Oregon. Pahto, with his head bent toward his love, became what we call Mount Adams across the river in Washington. Loowit became what we call Mount St. Helens, also in Washington. All three are active volcanoes. St. Helens famously erupted in 1980, the most destructive volcanic event in U.S. history.

The Ingenious Hidalgo—page 79

The epigraph is from faithful sidekick Sancho Panza in Cervantes' *El Ingenioso Hidalgo Don Quijote de la Mancha* [*The Ingenious Gentleman Don Quixote of La Mancha*].

The Barflies Discuss the King's Impending Visit—page 80

All the denizens of the imaginary Hoodoo Bar and Grill are tricksters from the stories of various cultures. Acme Inc. is a reference to the Road Runner cartoons. Robin Goodfellow is another name for the mischievous English jester Puck. John the Conqueroo is a crafty character of African-American folklore. In Greek mythology, Prometheus famously stole fire from the gods for humans to use, one incident in his dispute with Zeus; another was tricking the prime Olympian by serving him up a heap of bull's bones wrapped in a thin veneer of glistening meat. Anansi is the clever spider of West African folklore whose stories were brought to the Americas by enslaved Africans and who became a symbol of resistance. B'rer Rabbit, or Brother Rabbit, is the trickster hare of African folklore who also migrated along with enslaved Africans to the Americas; some of his adventures were collected by the U.S. folklorist Joel Chandler Harris in his Uncle Remus stories of the late 1800s. As to Tom Sawyer's picket fence whitewashing scheme—enough said. Good Soldier Schweik is the title character from the Czech writer Jaroslav Hašek's comic novels from the 1920s about a bumbling soldier whose seeming idiocy hilariously thwarts and exposes official incompetence and hypocrisy. Reynard the Fox is a European trickster whose stories date back to the Middle Ages, and Coyote is the famous Native American trickster. Finally, Oona McCool is the wife of the Irish mythological character Finn McCool; in one story, she saves Finn from a marauding giant by cooking griddle-irons into some cakes so the giant will break his teeth when he gobbles them down.

A Minnesota Boy—page 96

Sonja Heinie was an internationally-famous Norwegian figure skater who won gold medals at three Olympics in the 1920s and 30s and later made a long career with touring ice shows and in the movies. "Gold" refers to Gold Beach, the World War II code name for one of the five Allied landing areas in Normandy during the D-Day invasion of German-occupied France in 1944.

The Choice—page 100

Caryl Chessman was a career criminal sentenced to death for a series of horrible kidnappings and rapes in Los Angeles in 1948. He spent almost twelve years on Death Row, the longest span ever there in the U.S. at the time, during which his case became a centerpiece of national death penalty debates. Exhausting all his appeals, Chessman died in the San Quentin gas chamber. When the cyanide pellets dropped into the acid bucket beneath the seat into which he was strapped, witnesses said Chessman held his breath as long as he could.

Czechoslovakia: July 20, 1969—page 101

In the summer of 1969, I visited what was then Czechoslovakia with my future wife Jan Giske (while we were both college students in Germany) less than a year after a Soviet invasion crushed the reform-minded government there.

I Can't Breathe—page 105

In New York City in 2014, an unarmed black man named Eric Garner, complaining about being arrested, was thrown to the ground by a police officer using a chokehold. With five officers restraining him, Garner said "I can't breathe" eleven times as he was handcuffed face down on the sidewalk. He lost consciousness, remained untended on the ground for seven minutes before an ambulance arrived, and was pronounced dead at a hospital an hour later. Garner's crime: selling cigarettes illegally.

Citizen's United—page 106

Citizen's United vs. Federal Election Commission was the 2010 U.S. Supreme Court decision which held that the free speech clause of the First Amendment prohibits laws restricting expenditures for political campaigning—in essence treating the pouring of money into elections by corporations, unions, and special interest groups as the equivalent of individuals exercising their free speech rights.

A Christmas Song After Listening to a Children's Choir—page 115

This poem was partly inspired by watching an online video of the choir from Killard House, a school for students with special needs in Donaghadee, Northern Ireland. Led by then-10-year-old Kaylee Rogers, who has autism, the choir performs alternative lyrics to Leonard Cohen's "Hallelujah."

Acknowledgements

Grateful acknowledgement goes to the publications where these poems first appeared, sometimes in earlier forms.

Clackamas Literary Review: "Cassandra in Three Acts," "Dirtwork: The Spring Campaign," "The Old Men of Argos"

Cloudbank: "Daphne by the Front Steps," "Do You Ever," "Fractions"

English Journal: "End of the Season," "For the Group Under the Table," "Ode to My Student's Pen," "Save," "Teacher as King Kong"

Northwest Magazine: "Yardwork"

Oregon English Journal: "City Nature," "The Janitor" (originally published as "Sarge"), "Spider Plant," "Two-Year-Old Shirtless in the Garden..." (originally published as "Nathan the Blackberry Boy"), "Up Eagle Creek Trail"

The Oregonian: "Finding Direction"

The Poeming Pigeon: "Citizens United"

Timberline Review: "After Act V," "What Shall I Sing?"

Windfall: A Journal of Poetry of Place: "Bucking Hay for Pat," "On Sandy Boulevard," "Out on a Record-Breaking Warm Saturday," "That Day at the Hat Shop"

"A Hesitant Love Poem to Second Period English on the Occasion of Valentines Day" first appeared in *A Ritual to Read Together: Poems in Conversation with William Stafford*, edited by Becca J.R. Lachman, Woodley Press, Topeka: 2013

Gratitude

I am immeasurably thankful to...

...Kim Stafford, for a long history of encouragement and friendship rooted in story-fueled rambles on the backroads of Oregon.

...Lana Hechtman Ayers, for pitching to me the idea of this collection and being such a supportive, efficient, and patient editor.

...Jerry Sprout, for his enthusiasm and writerly advice on many Stumptown Stomps, and Janine Sprout, for her consultations and contributions to the cover.

...Veronica Paracchini, whose lively laugh we sorely miss and whose spirit hovers over this whole project.

...Jim Johnsrud, ace neighbor, for carting his little library around in a red wagon, helping me think about books and photos and angles.

...Walt, Emily, Robert, W.C., Langston, Theodore, Maya, Adrienne, Gwendolyn, Gary, and Lawrence, for your words.

...Jan, Nate, Kate, Marlowe, Josh, Jenna, Tevyn, and Shawnie: these are the names indelibly tattooed on my heart.

About the Author

For many decades, poems have been leaking from Tim Gillespie's brainpan, leaving marks along the roads of his wanderings.

In fifth grade, he was moved by no assignment to write a rhyming poem on the occasion of his younger brother's birth. He showed it to his teacher in his hometown. Without telling him, the teacher submitted it to a contest at the Los Angeles County fair. Some weeks later, his family found the poem thumb-tacked with scores of others on a display board at the back end of a vast animal husbandry hall filled with roosters, pigeons, goats, and rabbits. Few people were back there to see the blue ribbon, but amid the bleats and clucks in the heart of the L.A. megalopolis, he found some of the essentials of his poetry: serendipity, juxtaposition, the music of sound, and the glory of an art that no one performs or publishes for wide acclaim or money, only for love.

At the age of 18, the author left Southern California in an old station wagon to attend Stanford University, where he majored in English, helping pay his way with jobs as a warehouseman, parts truck driver, and merchant seaman. He married Jan Giske right out of college, then took a job as an aide at an inner-city elementary school in Oakland, California, to fulfill his two-year alternative service obligation as a conscientious objector to the Vietnam War. Though he originally thought he would pursue journalism, that experience hooked him on a teaching life.

Moving with his wife to Portland, Oregon, the author got his teaching credential and began an almost-forty-year public school career, mostly teaching high school English. He has been President of the Oregon Council of Teachers of English, a founding co-director of the Oregon Writing Project at Lewis & Clark College, and one of the original founders of the annual Oregon Writing Festival for student writers, a statewide extravaganza that for over 30 years has attracted almost a thousand young writers annually to participate in a day of workshops and readings. A winner of a National High School English Teacher of Excellence Award from the National Council of Teachers of English, he wrote regularly about his experiences during his years in the classroom. Nearly 100 of his essays, articles, and chalkdust poems have appeared in national educational publications and books, and he is the author of his own thick book for teachers, *Doing Literary Criticism*, published by Stenhouse Press.

At the same time, he and his wife raised two sons and now have two much-loved daughters-in-law and a collection of terrific grandchildren. An avid reader, walker, hiker, and traveler (often to his wife's ancestral homeland of Norway), he played harmonica and wrote lyrics for many years for the late, slightly-lamented blues-rock band Big Blind.

Through all these adventures and activities, the author found poems adding sense, wonder, and music to life.

CPSIA information can be obtained
at www.ICGtesting.com
Printed in the USA
LVHW110209220721
693377LV00004B/397